"GUYS ARE SCHMUCKS!"

A Woman's Guide to Surviving... & Enjoying Men

Laura d'Angelo, MD
Bob Richardson

Cold Tree Press

Author Photo by Alex Loosen

Published by Cold Tree Press
Nashville, Tennessee
www.coldtreepress.com

To my two favorite guys,
my sons,
Alex and Max

"Every woman should read this before she even thinks about getting married."

— Jackie Hunter
Single mother and caregiver

"This book hits on points that are very, very relevant to us men, and it's a reality rarely exposed. It's a source of enlightenment for women so they understand the men in their lives more, and a source of satisfaction for men as we desire to be known. It's highly satisfying to read this book and feel we are known."

— Michael Mariano
Entrepreneur

"I think women and men should read this book and realize that not all men are schmucks all their lives. That everyone makes mistakes and a successful marriage or relationship depends upon the ability to give and forgive each other and strive on. I think men still want to pursue and women want to be pursued. Where have all the gentlemen gone to? Men really do want to be treated as kings and they want to treat their ladies as queens. Just give us time and a chance."

— Douglas Owens
Truck driver, RDF Logistics

WARNING:
"Guys Are Schmucks!" is insightful, useful,
controversial, R-Rated, and down-right Schmucky.

GRATITUDE GOES TO...

*Suzanne, who teaches me everything
she knows about men.
To Al, for his attempts to educate me about men.
To Bob, whose love for me led me to believe
some of the things he sees in me.
To all the guys who so spontaneously,
and with trust, confided in me.*

TABLE OF CONTENTS

A FOREWORD
BY JUDY ANDREWS

The first man I ever loved (and whom I have loved the longest) was, and is, my father. My daddy is an honorable man and a pillar of the community. The other men I've loved as long as I can remember are my three brothers, all as honest as the day is long. Growing up in a nuclear family of mythologically-honest folks, I didn't know about schmucks until too late. As my father would say, "Not only did I know nothing about schmucks, I didn't even suspect nothing!" My mother was an equal to my father, and he took pains to make sure we children knew it. We were respectful of our parents, and they earned our respect every day.

Flash forward. A few decades have passed. One fateful night, twenty years after I married Mr. Right and three children later, my house burned down. Immediately, I start coping by trying to make our three children's lives normal while grieving and replacing everything we ever owned. My husband is working longer hours and more nights than ever before, trying to stay on top and pull down the bucks to put three girls through college, not to mention pay for some weddings, we hope. He has replaced his Porsche Boxster convertible (the one he bought as soon as the first model came out), the one whose bumper slightly melted in the fire. It's summer, our girls are away at camp, and I've been trying to rekindle the romance in our marriage, since the grief and chaos after the house burned down seemingly put a crimp in that department of our marriage. It's Friday night, and my husband and I have a movie date, but he doesn't come home until 8:30 PM, a little late for a 7 PM movie, our standard movie time. "What gives?" I want to know. And the schmuck rears his ugly head, "I've been unfaithful," he says. After months of therapy, both together and separately, I discover that the schmuck is in love with a woman (yeah, 12 years younger and skinnier to boot) that he has been seeing for almost a year.

Since becoming a victim of adultery and dishonesty, not to mention being devastated by someone who was supposed to love me supremely, I've had a quick, dirty course in schmuckdom. As I've gravitated to other women who are divorcing, too (surprise, surprise!), I've heard legendary stories of schmuckdom. My father and my brothers were quick to confirm that, guess what, all men are schmucks.

So, parents, gal pals, wives and husbands, make this book a primer for the girls and women in your lives.

If you're a man, choose to be honorable, but share with the women you love the truth about naturally testosterone-laden schmucks. Spare them from finding out the hard way, like I did. Heed this book.

Knowing the finer points of schmuckdom will prepare girls and women and guys of all ages to talk honestly about the drive of men to one-up fellow men and to feed their egos. This book won't revolutionize relationships, and it might not save marriages, but it will give girls and women insider knowledge about the urges and the motivations of men. ("Forewarned is forearmed," another saying from my dad.) This knowledge won't deprive men of their need to be powerful and to dominate their worlds any more than a tell-all book about women would wipe out their urges to nurture and shop. But "Guys Are Schmucks" will give women and men a common language to talk about the challenges of relationships between a schmuck and a woman. Knowledge is power. Use this book, and share it, or better yet, buy copies for the females you love!

– Judy Andrews
May, 2004
Nashville, TN

INTRODUCTION

Dr. Laura was in Portland, Oregon working on a project. A script was keeping me busy in Nashville. Laura and I had been friends for several years and had written a couple of Hollywood screenplays. We talked by phone at least once a week.

After a lengthy conversation one day Laura said, "Bob, 'Guys Are Schmucks!' How's that for the title of a book?"

"Are you nuts?!" I bellowed.

Amused, Laura replied, "I've interviewed several guys here in Portland and they like it."

Surprised, thinking Laura was pulling a gag, I growled, "I'd forget it. It won't sell. SCHMUCK to a guy means a real loser – an A #1 jerk."

Laura cut in, "Bob, the guys get a charge out of it. You won't believe this, but they're all telling me what schmucks they've been."

When Laura returned to Nashville with the first batch of interviews I read the raw material. I was amazed at what these guys were telling her. In revealing their 'schmucky' side, they were unwittingly revealing the side of a man's world which women don't fully understand.

Every woman should read and reread this book. It will give every woman the opportunity to take full advantage of getting to know the complete man. Once understood, a woman will be better able to accept him just as he is without trying to change him.

This is the answer to living with a ~~schmuck~~ *guy*.

— Bob Richardson
August 2003
Nashville, TN

ORIGINS

"Laura, I've found your soul mate." So spoke Frank, a male psychiatric colleague who was encouraging me to date now that I was divorced after nearly 20 years of marriage.

Just the words to catch my attention. "Really, who is he?"

"He's about your age. Never married. Has dated a lot of women, but only one at a time. Then he breaks it off when she wants to get married. He has a teenage daughter from an earlier relationship and he's a good father. I've known him about twenty years. I think you two would really get along. He has a great sense of humor. You're both from New York."

An active playboy who has left a trail of broken hearts. "Frank, is this a joke? Why would you want to set me up with a guy like that?"

Frank stopped what he was doing to look me straight in the eye, "Laura, let me tell you something. All guys are schmucks. If you can learn to accept that, you'll do fine."

Hmm, not exactly the words I expected, much

less wanted, to hear. But when I brought this up in conversations with male friends during the next few months each and every one of them agreed with Frank. And each and every one started telling me about their personal experiences as a schmuck. I was surprised that they were not offended. In fact, the topic led to spontaneous and unusual conversations. Men were comfortably telling me about themselves and enjoying it. At 47, I figured I had something to learn. Hence, these conversations were the springboard which led to more formal interviews and this book was birthed.

Over the next eighteen months I interviewed American men whose ages ranged from 17 to 85. I was amazed and encouraged by how willing men were to reveal their most private thoughts. "It was cleansing," one gentleman enthusiastically told me. The only men who were hesitant to be interviewed were those men I previously knew stating, "If I tell you the truth, I'm afraid you won't like me." The exception was my son who volunteered to be interviewed, stating, "I'll tell you everything you need to know as long as you don't abuse your power."

Although their education and professions were diverse, I noticed recurrent themes and patterns between all of them. These consistent patterns became the categories from which the chapters developed and a blueprint emerged of what makes a guy a guy. I found that the chapters represented the developmental stages through which men evolve.

God knows women never stop talking about men. But let's face it, do we really know men? Do we listen to them? Who better to learn about men than from the men themselves? With that said, I've made every effort to keep my voice out of it.

And maybe, just maybe, along the way we can learn to understand, accept and enjoy men just as they are. Frankly, I think men would be relieved and grateful. Note that I didn't say "love" them. We seem to do that too readily with a bunch of drama, frustration, and heartache. Perhaps that's our problem. Not many women I know talk about *enjoying* men.

I discovered one very surprising thing when I first set out to do the interviews. Guys figured women already knew the stuff they were telling me about themselves because, as they told me, "We are born of a woman; she's the original truth and protection and that stays with us the rest of our lives." Men don't see themselves as mysterious or complicated. How much do we let our femininity color our judgement of the male?

In spite of our female intuition, we still have some very basic things to learn about guys. As one gentleman said, "Women have heard this stuff, but they just don't want to believe it."

**N.B. All names have been changed to
protect the guilty**

"GUYS ARE SCHMUCKS!"

A Woman's Guide to Surviving... & Enjoying Men

Laura d'Angelo, MD
Bob Richardson

Chapter 1

WHAT EVERY GUY TOLD ME

"Sure, I'd be glad to be interviewed. Most guys are schmucks." I heard it over and over again. In a very unscientific fashion, according to the guys, the percentage of schmucks among them ranged from a low of 40% to a high of 99%. Whatever the percentage may be, they all said, "it's extremely high….that's our role model." Wow!

And, oddly enough, not a single guy asked me what I meant by a schmuck. Not a single guy asked me to define a schmuck. Indeed, the very next thing they did was tell me what a schmuck is. They just hit the ground running as if they intuitively knew. I learned early on that "guys don't take offense at names." As one said, "Call him a redneck, he's proud of it. Call him a hillbilly, he's proud of it." And it seems that 'schmuck' was also a term that didn't cause them to take offense.

So, what exactly is a schmuck? Well, to begin with, animal analogies were common. "Trust me, for the most part, all men are pigs." "There's a little bit of dog in each of us." "A little bit?" I was corrected by another guy. Below is a list of the definitions men gave.

A schmuck is a guy who:

- doesn't respect women
- doesn't like women
- doesn't appreciate the power of a woman
- is married and wants to play both sides of the fence
- is unmarried and wants to date six different women who don't know about each other
- finds some chippy somewhere and breaks up his family to marry her. That's a schmuck! (this was a universal opinion)
- gets so crazy about something – golf, hunting, a woman – that everything else is nothing
- believes his own publicity
- blames others for the valleys in his life
- must be at his mother's house on Friday (without you) – it means he hasn't cut the cord
- if you lean on his car, he takes out a handkerchief to wipe it
- brings his friend along on a date. That's a putz. There'll be no intimacy or love-making because he's got a buffer
- doesn't shut his cell phone off while having an intimate dinner
- says he's low maintenance (that's a euphemism for "I'm going to live exactly as I did before I knew you")

- breaks the law because he's gambling with his life and being locked up is worse than death.
- pulls the wool over a woman's eyes, making her think she's wonderful until he gets what he wants.
- flips his values for quick pleasure
- knows better but doesn't do better
- is pretty low on the moral scale. It's not just a matter of morality with women. It's a matter of ethics. It's how ethical you are in business dealings. It's how you act in college when you take an exam. It's not just a matter of cheating on your wife.

As you can already see, I was told some very powerful things about guys. Puting this list together, nonetheless, caused me to catch my breath and take pause. I felt I was drowning in schmuckdom. Just when I thought I could hear no more, a 74-year-old man in one of the last interviews told me, "Yeah, 99% of guys are schmucks. But I may be over killing it. You see, we all do schmucky things. But if you're talking about 'once a schmuck, always a schmuck, I'd say it's 5%.'" So, it's likely that nearly all guys will qualify as schmucks during their lives, but it's not a permanent condition.

Women. Women were discussed everywhere and throughout the interviews. Men ranked women ahead of men in terms of just about everything related to love, emotionality, and power – the ultimate power being love. A woman can't change a guy, but she can "motivate and inspire a man. The beauty of a woman is her nurturing, her love, and her faithfulness. True femininity is gentle strength. She has conviction, character, and tenderness. True femininity is so strong."

I thought back to years ago when as a teenager I watched newly elected President Nixon introduce his Cabinet (of men) on television. The wives stood proudly in the background as he said that old adage, "Behind every successful man is a woman." After listening to men this year and a half I'm beginning to understand what he truly meant.

So, back to the matter at hand and let's take a look at what guys said about themselves through their lifespan.

Chapter 2

BOYHOOD: PRANKSTERS, RASCALS & RISK-TAKERS

Boys will be boys. We've all heard that. How about "men will be boys," as told to me by a 20-year-old? That garnered a laugh from everyone present at the discussion. But it was the 17-year-old who properly redirected me when he told me that "men *are* boys." So, if manhood is rooted, if not stuck, in boyhood, let's start at the beginning.

The first ten years of life, as nature intended, are mommy oriented, focused, and dependent. A combination of expected things happen ranging from survival to young men finding themselves picking up family and social values. As boys grow, they change, make decisions, get into trouble here and there, break rules--they are sort of testing limits. One 46-year-old reflected, "This is probably the decade where they do this ruckus – or schmuck stuff – on purpose. Cause if I do this schmuck stuff I may be the center of attention." They don't really know or care where the attention will come from, but they hope to be the focus of it.

Here is the first glimmer of the distinctions between boys and girls. **Breaking rules and pushing limits**

are 'highs' for a guy. It's pretty much how boys spend their childhood because it was with a smirk, a glimmer in their eye, and finally a knowing glance as if they were looking directly into their past, that guy after guy readily recalled their boyhood antics. One 79-year-old put it succinctly, "Boys are crazy! I wonder why I'm still alive!" He recalled that at the tender age of five he used to put nails under the tires of the landlady's car.

Another gentleman told me without hesitation, "Little boys are a bundle of misdirected energy. They want to hit, knock things over, and run. They have no thought pattern. They'd run into a brick wall cause the other guy did it. But boys are fun."

Doorbell ditch seemed to be a universal activity. "We went around ringing doorbells at night. Whoever could ring the doorbell and hide as close to the door as possible without getting caught would be the winner." That seemingly harmless prank could be upgraded to include an uncovered jar of urine leaning against the door so it would readily spill over when the innocent home owner opened the door. Or the nastier version of placing a burning bag of doggie fecal matter at the door hoping that the home owner would stomp it out with his foot leaving him not just angry but redolent in the worst sort of way. I was not sure if any of the guys actually succeeded in fooling anyone to knock over a jar of urine or stomp on the bag, but the guys sure liked to tell me about it. Just the thought of such a prank gave them a charge.

Other thrills involved distracting and startling unsuspecting drivers in hopes of stopping traffic and thereby causing chaos. One method would be to stage a horrific accident in the street. "We'd take two crumpled up bikes, and one of us would lay under the bikes as if he was seriously injured. When a car would stop we'd all get up and run away." Or building, for example, a leaf fort in the street and placing a coat in the middle of it to look like a dead body waiting for a driver to stop to see if someone had been killed. "Most people, though, would drive right over it." This lack of reaction was an obvious disappointment.

The point here is that it's a thrill just to get something to happen. "We used to entertain ourselves for days at a time – like what would happen if we ran down the street naked…if we did this or that." The reaction is more important than what he does to get that reaction. Just get it to happen…there's the fun.

The holy grail is dropping anything off a building from a high place, even hocking a big loogey. "I still to this day sometimes spit down a staircase," 40-year-old Mr. M told me. "If you could possibly break a window you'd feel good for a week." Mr. B remembered back nearly 70 years ago when he was "the best sling-shot guy. I shot the street lights out and broke a row of garage windows. It made the headlines in the local paper and I never got caught. At my 50th school reunion my friend asked me if I remembered this. The others got caught and went to jail! I didn't remember that part."

Some risky play was purposely done without an audience because the boys knew it was downright dangerous and would be forbidden if parents learned about it. "We used to go walking on a narrow ledge that circled the third story of a building, just for the fun of it. We couldn't have been more than 8-years-old." The same 86-year-old gentlemen recalled when he was about ten his family lived on the north side of Chicago near the shore of Lake Michigan. "In the winter the lake would freeze out to about four hundred yards. If the winds were unusually strong, the waves would freeze into all sorts of unusual convolutions. We used to go out on there and crawl through the ice caves. We could also see the water where the ice had parted. We knew it was dangerous – that added the zest to the whole thing."

As the boyhood years inched closer to the teenage years the thrills get more grandiose and downright dangerous, making the excitement even greater and the prize of impressing the other kids much more valuable. One guy recalled the summer he was twelve which was highlighted by his putting on 'fire shows' for the neighborhood kids. He would pour puddles of gasoline in front of the garage and light a match to them to the enjoyment and wonderment of his friends. He spent the rest of the summer sitting in the charred remains of the burned garage as ordered by his dad.

Another unintentional disaster was recalled by an 80-year-old who described how he and his buddies would go to the local lumber yard where the lumber was stacked about 15 to 18 feet high. "We'd climb up and jump from one stack to another. It was too high to land on your feet, so we'd land on our whole body. I don't know how we didn't kill ourselves. There was also a huge shed of bunches of wooden shingles and we'd burrow in there and make tunnels. I wonder why we weren't crushed to death. I had my first cigarette down there while reading SPICEY DETECTIVE and the book caught fire. We almost burned down the entire lumber yard that day. Incidentally, that was my last cigarette."

This same kinetic energy directed towards the outside world also happens between young boys. "Boys fight. They'll fight even their best friends. They have to fight. It's in their genes. You gotta see who's tougher. Girls will get you with words, but guys will fight. It's over in a minute, on the ground, bloody nose. Boys will look for weakness in other guys. Little boys will spot a mommy's boy and attack. If a guy pushes you around, and you fight back, even if you lose, they'll leave you alone...as long as you fight back." I asked how long that lasts. Mr. S continued without hesitation, "Oh, that stays. Guys enjoy putting ourselves on top and putting other people down." And it seems to happen amongst best friends. Perhaps it's determining the hierarchy? Perhaps it's the first inkling of a guy staking out his territory?

Whatever it is, pay attention, because you will see that the prankster, rascal and daredevil in a boy is the impulsive energy that will stay with a guy in the years ahead. And here is where women can start to understand guys. They're out there, in your face. Lots of action, not much talk. Masculine aggression is part and parcel of being male. Boys like to lock horns, butt heads, and do all those Tarzan things that put them in the path of danger. This same aggression continues throughout the life span. It will express itself differently later in life, but the instinct will be the same. "It's what builds skyscrapers, sends men to the moon, declares war, creates and raids corporations."

Sure, schmuckdom starts young and boys are crazy, but the operative phrase is *"Boys are fun."*

Chapter 3
TEENAGERS: THE VICE SQUAD AND PROUD OF IT

The testosterone surge at around 12 or 13 years catapults the mischievous boy into the teenager. Prior to the hormonal rush, his antics were fun. Now they step up the action with vandalism, alcohol, drugs, pornography, and sex.

In the teenage years being schmucky is a kind of "posturing – creating the definition of who you are. There is good stuff, too – like being an Eagle Scout, but the schmucky stuff carries equal weight. It helps to create your image." Uncontrolled trouble is fun and there is the reward of watching the adults react to it, but those joys are secondary. Teenagers aren't doing this stuff just to get random attention. Rather, in the inimitable words of one teenager, "That's just the way we are." Well, let's see.

Vandalism. Teenage vandalism is blithely considered spare time fun. "You do it 'cause you laugh when you do it." There's what's called petty vandalism, like firecrackers in the mailbox, or taking the air out of the neighbor's tire. And then there's a little thievery here and there. "Mr. Jones kept four cases of beer in his garage. When he wasn't around we'd borrow a couple of bottles."

There's always one house where the teenage gang congregates. "One kid's mom was a flaming alcoholic, worked as a nurse at night, slept all day, no food in the house, no dad. My friend had a Simca car. It didn't run, but was parked in the garage and when we were really bored we'd take turns behind the wheel and push the car around the neighborhood. It was all an attention getting thing. We wanted to be seen as guys doing something, even if it was wrong. We were smart-assed pranksters." The thrill is to get something to happen. "I used to bet guys that they wouldn't go streaking. When I was about 14 (he's now 40) you could get a guy to streak through McDonald's for $5.00."

The previous examples were mild compared to how annoying some ideas could be. "When we were about 15 or 16 we used to go to the country club about ten or eleven o'clock at night to play golf. We'd crap in the cup and put the flag back in. Years later I was golfing with a local politician, and his ball went 'glump' into the cup. I knew exactly what had happened. The senator started screaming, 'They should be arrested! What kind of an animal would do this?' I couldn't stop laughing." Definitely guy stuff. Would you ever hear of a teenage girl pulling such a stunt? Females don't like using public toilets, never mind even thinking that it would be humorous to do so at the local putting green.

One gentleman in his 80's recalled his college years at Northwestern University in the 1930's. He and his school friends used to go down to Notre Dame for football games or weekend parties. "A group of us drunk guys would go down to the trolley cars at night and lift them off the tracks, just to fuck the whole thing up." To the delight of the offending vandals, traffic was held up for a couple of days while a large construction crane was brought in at great cost to lift the trolley back on its tracks.

Mailbox bashing can be considered the gold standard as it surfaced as the most common and most fun of all the possible acts of vandalism. "You just kinda hear people talk about it, so it makes it a tradition. It stays in a certain age group; 16 to 18 is the prime age range. **It could be considered a form of male bonding for a lot of reasons.** It's fun, you need teamwork, it's funny, it's a federal offense, it's in front of the victim's house, it's extremely loud, and it's pretty violent. The stakes are high so that makes it even better. It's like wham, bam, thank you m'am." I was told that you pick anonymous mailboxes. "If you do it to someone you know, it's a dick thing. You're making a statement." The weapon of choice is a Little League aluminum baseball bat. "It's small, easy to use, it's rugged, durable, it's extremely cheap, and it will last you your entire youthful career."

Teenagers told me there are websites where people submit vandalism ideas. Put LSD on a door handle so it will be absorbed through the skin. WD40 on the car windshield. There you have it. Vandalism is raised from an art to a science in the teenage years.

Teenage girls may not practice vandalism as teenage boys do, but to a guy the power of gossip is as potent as vandalism. "Guys don't spread rumors about other guys the way girls do. We talk about girls, but it's not like a rumor. The bottom line is that girls spread more rumors and gossip than guys do. We have vandalism and that's obviously bad, but girls have their own version."

Pornography. Between the ages of 12 and 14 guys start discovering pornography. As one teenager told me, *"Every* single guy has had his fair share of pornography. One guy had his trunk filled with porno magazines. The distinguishing feature is the sheer volume. That's just the way it is. That'll never change. Kids have their own underground industry. They like to trade. There's always the one guy who is the ring leader and in charge. You know who's gonna be a wheeler-dealer at just 14."

Sex. Just about all of the men interviewed had their first sexual experiences during their teenage years. Interestingly enough, the men who came of age before the 'sexual revolution' of the 1960's, those who are now about 60-years and older, learned about sex from 'an older woman'. She may have been in her 20's, or even 30's, but back then that really seemed older. And because sex was more of a taboo and society expected discretion about these youthful indiscretions, their early encounters were clandestine, risky, and frankly, outrageous even by today's standards. Listen to what a few of the older gents said.

Mr. B, now 68, grew up in Mississippi. "When I was a sophomore in high school I made it with my history teacher. She came on to me. I was sitting at my desk. We were taking a test and it was my habit to hold the clipboard. I was in the very back of the room and she straddled my fist with her crotch. No one else could see it. She was about 35. I was about 17. At the end of the class she announced that she was doing some housework at her house and was there a boy in the class who could help her and I volunteered. I went there on Saturday. It went on for a while until she moved to Florida that summer. Her friend told me she thought she had been attracted to the high school football coach and followed him down there. Many years later she retired and came back to my hometown. I went to a high school reunion hoping she would show up, but she didn't. I was told she had developed Alzheimer's."

Another story which took place about fifty years ago followed the same pattern: innocent male youth encounters female pedagogue willing to impart her knowledge. "There was a teacher in another school, a rural school. She drove into the drive-in restaurant where I was with my two cousins. She had another woman with her. She feigned interest in my car. She said there was something wrong with her car, and asked me if I could drive it with her. We went out immediately and parked and had sex. I was 17. She was in her 30's."

"When I was a freshman in college about fifty years ago I dated a local high school girl. She was away visiting a nearby college one weekend and was due home that Sunday night. I went to her home and her mother greeted me. She was drinking scotch and she offered me a drink while we were watching TV. The daughter called to say the bus was snowbound and they wouldn't make it back that night. After a few more scotches, the mother and I went to bed together. It was wonderful! She knew all the things to do. She was better and more experienced. That was the first time I had done it in a bed…not the back seat of a car. And the first time the woman had been completely nude. It was a marvelous experience. The mother didn't want me screwing her daughter. Another time, while the girl was getting ready for our date the mother and I made it on the washing machine. I thought the woman was wonderful. Do you think a man can ever forget that?"

One man grew up in New York and Chicago back

in the 1930's. "Most of the families in my neighborhood had housekeepers from Eastern Europe. Invariably, my friends and I all learned about sex from these women. When I was 15, I remember seeing voluptuous Louisa in the kitchen and she came on to me. We used to slosh around in the car in the garage. Later on I used to share her with two other friends of mine."

My favorite story, because it is the most outrageous, was told to me by a 60-year-old. He and his friend Paul were both 19 when Paul urged him to take a ride to the coast to take a look at a boat that he had seen in the classifieds. "We went to this lady's house to look at it. We were standing in the kitchen talking about the boat and Paulie looks at the woman and says, 'Hey suck my cock right now.' She dove down and gave him a blow job. Then she gave me a blow job. It turns out that buying the boat was a ploy. Paul had been seeing her for a while. The next night there was a bunch of guys at her house and she blew everybody. Everybody had a ball. She was in control. She directed the whole thing. She and Paul went on for a couple of months."

Teenagers I interviewed were more guarded about sharing the details of their current sexual pursuits. That's understandable because it was these same young men who jokingly asked me not to abuse my power as they revealed their secret lives to me. But it's clear that they are discovering sex with their female peers. I didn't hear a single story about learning the ropes from an 'older woman'. I didn't get the blow by blow details from the teenagers, but grown men with teenage daughters did not hesitate to tell me just how they'll handle the boy their daughter wants to date, "I'd bring the guy in...I'm worried about her physical safety. I'd meet the boy and tell him I have a shot gun and a shovel and nobody would miss you."

Guys are very aware of their developing gender roles and what girls think about them. But, for the most part, "Guys talk about the way chicks look, that's about it. We don't have a complex mind." A 17-year-old noted that "Girls are complicated and they know that they're more complicated than men. Because of that they feel they're mentally superior to guys. They think they can change men. I'm not sexist, I'm not saying they're not smarter than men. Basically they think that men are simple and therefore can control us and think they can change us. Just 'cause we're simple doesn't mean we're stupid."

As I listened to all the seemingly outrageous stories I was at first horrified. Then I learned that *all* teenage guys have done, are doing, and will continue to do the same outrageous stuff. As I witnessed my 17-year-old son get his first speeding ticket and have his first car accident (as did all of his friends that year) it dawned on me that this stuff is universally male. *The very behaviors that horrify women are the very same behaviors that define masculinity to a guy.* And until the last couple of decades most of the authority figures that the teenagers faced when they appeared in court, the judges and lawyers, have been men who did the very same things in their youth. It is only since women's lib that many of the authority figures these boys now face are females who impose their own female brand of behavior which, I am learning, is radically different than the male's.

In the inimitable words of a 46-year-old who could have been speaking for every guy who described his teenage years, "Don't bother trying to reason or talk about those years because the definition of teenage schmuckdom is that you think you know everything. Make no mistake about it. A teenage guy knows everything. And because of that he's not going to take anybody's opinion to heart."

One last bit of wisdom about teenage guys. "Don't expect any teenager to tell you what's going on." Guys are not about talking. **Guys bond with their actions.** And they minimize everything. Girls, the drama queens that they are, maximize everything. With guys, you'll learn what's going on when the cops knock at the door or the grandbaby you didn't know you had shows up wrapped in swaddling clothes.

The good news is that the teenage years are self-limiting. Eventually, if a guy survives himself, he will turn 20.

No sooner did I finish that last sentence when the phone rang. It was my soon-to-be 21-year-old son telling me what he wanted for his birthday. "Mom, I know what you can get me for my birthday."

"Really? Ok, tell me. That'll save me some work."

"You can give me money so I can go sky diving."

"Over my dead body." And it probably will be.

Chapter 4
SCHMUCKY DATING:
WOMEN DATE, MEN HUNT

"...And they like to catch and release, too. Most men don't even know what dating is," I was told. Men are great hunters. They *all* told me that. "Every guy is looking for a hunt. He'll hunt until he kills that buck and he'll proudly mount it on his wall. Or that one fish that every man wants to catch. And once he catches it it's not as exciting."

So, when it comes to women, men are hunting for sex. And the above principles apply. Hunt, catch, and release. A guy will proudly go track it (sex) down, and beat the bushes until he finds it. I know this isn't easy for women to accept because if that's the object of the hunt, once caught and conquered he'll go on to the next catch. But, once understood, women will better understand some of the schmucky things guys do when women think they're 'dating' them.

For example, having sex with a guy is the beginning of a relationship for a woman. For the schmucky guy, becoming sexual with a woman can mark the end of the relationship. **The fun was in the challenge, and the challenge was the hunt.** I asked a 22-year-old why it so often seems that the guy hates you after he sleeps with you. "Well, they don't hate you for it. It's just that it's not the special woman for him. It's like going hunting – you wanna get that big buck, but if you don't you'll shoot a few doe – just to do it. It's not that special one, but you'll wanna bring something home." A 61-year-old bus driver, happily married for nearly 40 years stated, "A guy goes into a relationship to get laid and after that process the woman's feelings get more deeply involved. And once he's done, he don't care. It's the challenge." He emphatically went on, "I see it everyday on the bus with the young kids. I see these girls flirting. I try to tell them not to let that idiot fool you. He'll promise you anything to get your drawers off. Guys under-stand that men are schmucks. God made them that way. He gets into heat basically looking at a woman. It's not his fault. A little girl can show her under drawers and he's ready. A woman has got to have feel-ings to get involved, so he'll sweet talk her. Men have few feelings. Women need to understand and accept men for what they are so they don't get badly fooled."

A hunter can only hunt one thing at a time. "It's a male thing. We're so focused on one thing. Then we're on to the next thing." He may seem so entirely focused on you in the beginning and then, once bedded, that focus is lost. "When a man gets worked up it takes so much blood away from his brain that he can't think no more." So, when a woman thinks a man is infatuated with her it can just be the hunter focusing on his prey. As a side note, he told me this also explains why men are bad shoppers. "If I want a blue suit, I'll go to the store and look *only* for that blue suit. And when I find that suit I'll buy it. Women can shop for all sorts of things. Why do you think Tractor Supply Company is so popular? Because it has everything a man needs." As writer Ann Patchett notes, "Do men ever have a three hour lunch and then walk around looking in store windows as an excuse to just keep talking?"

Paralleling the hunter mentality is the herding instinct. **Men love a herd of women.** "Women are generally attracted to one man, but men can be attracted to many females. We can love many women at a time. We can't help it. A guy doesn't need to drop one woman for another." Or, simply put, "We like variety." Not only did every guy agree with this, but it was emphasized with "That's the most male thing there is. Men are attracted to a herd. It's always been that way and it's always going to be that way."

What makes a herd so attractive to a man? "It's easier to talk about the herd mentality. Then you don't have to deal with feelings." Guys don't show their feelings "Because they're afraid of them. If they have feelings they're vulnerable, and when they're vulnerable that's when they're afraid they're gonna be attacked." And one of those very potent feelings for a man is love. Women revel in being in love, but "For a guy, it means loss of control." And if there's one thing he fears, it's to *not* be in control. To illustrate this primal fear, I was told a story about a dog who, when caught in a bear trap, was attacked by male dogs. Well, human males have the same fear. When a guy is down that's when he's gonna be pummeled. Remember how boys will attack another boy to test his mettle? Any weakness or vulnerability, which to a man includes love, will really scare a guy.

To stay in control, men lie. And men lie all the time. In fact, they'll say anything to look better. "Because we don't want to show our weaknesses, we'll lie to protect ourselves. If you have bills you can't pay, you'll just say, 'It'll be all right, don't you worry about it'. I think women don't expect men to tell them the truth because men bullshit a lot. So many women have heard so many lies from men that they get conditioned."

Ok, guys hunt, herd, and lie. The following is a perfect example of how one schmuck demonstrates all of these traits.

"My cousin John used to put on a *'FREE MANDELA'* t-shirt, borrow a couple of puppies, and sit on the lawn at Saturday Market pretending to write poetry in one of those black and white composition notebooks. He had copied other people's poems in there but, of course, acted as if they were his. He would also read poems by Maya Angelou or Robert Frost telling girls the poem made him think about a special woman. The girls would gather around him like flies. The notebook was full of chicks' numbers. When he'd get a chick to his apartment he claimed he never watched TV. He kept his TV on a roller and would hide it in the closet. He looked at TV *all* the time when he was alone. He has a total commitment phobia. He's still single."

Thinking about John reminded me of the old adage, "If it's too good to be true, it usually is."

"Yeah, guys do hunt, that's exactly right," laughed one now happily married 52-year-old guy, as he reminisced about his past. "You know, we used to spot chicks and then tell our buddies, 'I bet I can catch her.' So you'd do whatever you had to do to have sex with her. The bad thing was that after you went through all the motions and finally had sex, sometimes she'd end up liking you. And all you wanted was sex, so you'd feel real bad about breaking it off 'cause you know you've already been a shit."

Sounds like breaking up is hard for the guy to do? Well, according to the guys it is. But don't be fooled. It's not that they don't want to break your heart, or that it hurts. Rather, "**Guys do stuff to make girls wanna break up with them.** We know we're assholes and so we want to put the responsibility and guilt on the woman." He'll be passive-aggressive, unreliable, forgetful, rude – whatever lousy behavior it takes to get the woman to end it. Guys will do anything not to be the one to break it off. It's almost as if they think they're doing damage control, "Get the woman to end it so she won't say horrible things about how I broke up with her. We hate it when women talk about us behind our backs. We don't want to be seen as schmucks."

Even if a guy is not trying to break up the relationship, he's a master at putting responsibility and guilt on the woman. A 33-year-old twice divorced man revealed, "Most men will flip the script. If a guy knows he's dead wrong, he'll make the woman think she's wrong. She'll end up crying and apologizing. I think it's a defense mechanism when we mess up. We feel relieved, 'Whew, I got away with that one.' Then we'll go on to the next disaster." In fact, to take it a step further, he went on to say, "If she really, truly loves you she'll say she's wrong." Less than that, he sees that woman as "too independent."

And yet, when all is said and done, men are fully aware of the double standard here. While a guys feels entitled to hunt, chase, release or string along several women in a herd of his very own, he'll be devastated if a woman gives him a dose of his own medicine. "There's not a man in the world alive who hasn't had that experience of 'she got over me'.

When a woman says you are the greatest thing in the world and then she finds another man, your ego will never permit you to go back to her. A woman will love one at a time. If she drops you for another guy it's completely devastating."

"Most guys know that the woman works harder at the relationship than the guy. Most relationships ain't 50/50. Most men like to control the finances and know where you are at all times. If they can't do that with you they'll find somebody else. I think women get into wanting to cook and clean for a man to show him what he's getting, but a man will take advantage of that. **A woman doesn't need to work so hard that she's losing herself.** A guy knows when a woman is working to impress him. It might run some men away because we realize what she wants ain't what he wants, and he's outta there!"

Along those same lines of not working so hard to catch a guy, a happily married 40-year-old told me, "The biggest turn-on for most of us is when a woman has her own agenda and goals. Go out and buy a fucking house! Don't chase me. Let me catch up to you. I want to marry a woman who has something on the ball. I want a capable woman. The biggest turn on for me are those women who have good jobs – not a DFC (dumb, fucking cunt)."

Chapter 5
MARRIAGE

Mate fate – what a crapshoot! "Women need to realize that most guys are looking for a mate." It might not look that way depending upon the developmental stage of the guy you know, but ultimately – he's looking for a life partner.

Why do guys marry? Their answers surprised me. Women don't marry for the reasons the men gave. Responses ranged from laziness to convenience to convention and on up to nobility.

"A lot of men tend to marry out of laziness. This relationship is working, let's just do it."

"Security, pretty much. Guys get tired and bored with the dating scene. It's the right thing to do."

"I got married because I was so lonely. I was living with this wonderful woman, but our relationship was based purely on sex. But I needed to be loved."

"A guy gets married for the comfort of having somebody there most of the time. It makes things easier."

"A guy doesn't do well without a woman. We need some order in our lives and women give us that. Otherwise we're disorganized and we waste time."

"No guy is really happy unless he is providing for or taking care of someone. I feel more fulfilled, like I'm accomplishing something, protecting my family. I want my kids to grow up in a better environment."

"Most men have it in their hearts to have a woman and children to take care of. If a man doesn't have a woman he won't work as hard or as long. He's got to be working for *her*. He'll give her everything he can 'cause this is *his* woman. Take a look around at those who aren't married. They've got nothing and they don't care if they do. Eventually it hurts."

Men sixty and older frequently reported that they married because it was the conventional thing to do, "You get 21 and society says it's time for you to get married; usually after graduation."

When do guys start thinking about marriage? Well, guys who enter the workforce after high school start to grow up pretty quickly. Until that point a teenager doesn't think there is life after 19. "They're on such a high that everything is downhill after that." But after graduation either they "Keep on trucking with the lifestyle they had or they get on from there and start facing life. Once they start to learn to survive on their own, they see that life isn't that easy."

Guys who continue their education after high school also continue to sow their wild oats through their 20's. And then in their very early 30's they start thinking about money and a life companion (in that order). "After 30 you start looking at what makes guys macho and you see yourself getting older, gaining weight, and you can't compete with the 18-year-olds anymore. You realize you can't get the prettiest girl every time and you start to look at women differently. You think about compatibility. It's not just about their looks or sex. You start thinking 'what do I really want to do with my life and is this the woman to do it with?'"

What are some of the wrong reasons guys marry? Well, the younger and less mature the guy, the more likely he is to choose a mate for superficial reasons. For example, physical compatibility, wanting to be thought of as more mature than he is, or just plain competing with other guys. "The first time a guy has sex with a woman he's nervous. After it's done you don't have the same high unless it's the woman you're gonna marry. Then you have the same feeling." "Girlfriends come and go, but 'look at my wife.' Hey, she does everything for me…she's gorgeous…or has lots of money."

And the same guys told me that those are the very marriages that won't work. "Most divorces I see are in the 18 to 25-year-olds because they're both looking for that perfect life. They have a hard time compromising. They feel like they're giving up something. I was in the military at 17. Let me tell you, guys are animals in the barracks, happy animals 'cause they're all together, but animals. Most guys who married then ended up back in the barracks after three years, divorced 'cause 'she didn't do what I wanted her to do'. It's not until you're between 25 and 30 that you realize your wife is a person, too. Love is when you care more for your partner than you do for yourself. That's when it works. A lot of it is 'all about me' and it's getting to be more and more that way."

They either mature or find themselves divorcing over and over again. A guy will have a hard time compromising as long as he feels that marriage has forced him out of his carefree, self-centered life. "You realize you're not as perfect as you think you are. To make a marriage work you've got to realize whatever you thought was so great about you is not as great as you thought it was!"

What's at the heart of marriage? **Guy after guy told me that marriage is really about being with someone who is your companion.** As important as sex is, and it is *very* important, it is *not* the ultimate factor in choosing a partner. A 68-year-old man, married to his wife of 57 years said, "Marriage is not primarily a sexual relationship. It's sort of a life contract based on companionship. It's a lot more than sex. It becomes more binding, especially when the kids come along." This was echoed by a 40-year-old. "I dated a stunning model when I was 25. It was the best sex I ever had, but I didn't feel she was a great companion. My dad talked to me at that time about marriage. He told me that after 5 years the sex goes and that I'd better be with someone

who is my companion. And he is 100 percent right."
Lucky for this man and his wife of ten years who is his
great companion, he's still as horny at 40 as he was at
19. "Before we had kids we did it twice a day, morning
and night. But after the kids came it was once a day."
Nonetheless, that doesn't detract from his marriage.
Then, of course, there is the slightly more demanding
guy, "Every man wants his woman to carry herself well
– to be a lady in public. But in the bedroom he wants
her to be as freaky as possible. We want to have the best
of both worlds." He still hasn't found it as he is currently
single after two divorces.

What makes for a great companion? "Your goal
is to be able to have someone (your wife) you can tell
your true feelings to and get it all out and be accepted
for who you are. **A guy is only as good as his wife
thinks he is.** Since a guy doesn't talk with his friends
like women talk with their girlfriends the only person
a man can tell his true inner feelings to is his wife.
This 41-year-old went on, "A male ego is as fragile as
hell. A woman can tear him down with words, crush
him instantly, especially in front of other guys. If my
mate criticizes me, even if she's trying to help, it
crushes me. Any little thing she says can crush me."
Inside he's crushed, but outside he's gotta act tough.
"Women get to talk, get to cry with girlfriends.
Men can't do that with other guys."

What else makes a great companion for marriage?

"The more you have in common about your philosophy of life – raising kids, spirituality, your values – the better off the relationship. When you meet a guy don't think right away about the romantic stuff. Work on developing a friendship. Is this guy going to be a friend? That's the most important thing." "Guys want a lot of sex with a beautiful woman and they're happy! Oh, she should be intelligent, sweet, not too whiney, funny, and pretty. We don't care if she earns money, that's the guy's job. Don't get me wrong, a guy doesn't want a dumb blonde – it's an embarrassment to him. Because guys don't talk a lot they want a woman to talk, but not too much where she won't shut up. They want a good, loving woman."

"We both want our partner to be everything for us." A guy is very lucky if he finds someone who has realistic expectations. "Women just have to understand men and know where they're headed and not live in a fantasy world. Men are basically not socially gifted. They can be crude. Because they are not sensitive to subtle feelings, they can be awkward. A woman has to be in control. She has to lead the poor guy out of socially embarrassing situations without letting him know what she's doing."

The same guy had some very wise advice which, if we could all follow it, would serve us well. "There's not just one person you can marry. You could marry many people, but pick one and make it work."

Speaking of expecting your partner to be everything to you, guys know that "Every woman wants to remake a guy. If you're a drunk she wants to make you a preacher, if you're a preacher she wants to make you a drunk." It's the nature of the female to nurture, help things grow, and to create. But when this is carried over to re-creating a husband a wife is bound to run into resistance. "As soon as a woman gets you they want to change you. I know we're not couth, but that's how we're programmed." It was summed up beautifully when a guy told me, **"Love us for who we are and do not perceive us for who you want us to be."**

When a man marries he is at the peak of his potential. "A woman marries a guy thinking 'he's 90 percent of what I want and I can change the other 10 percent.' No, that's the peak, 90% is the most of what you'll get. *Who* you marry *when* you marry is the best of what you're going to get. After the wedding the woman will get less and less of what she wants. Guys get fatter, balder, and fartier. We're just plain. Women want us to be more complicated, but we ain't complicated. Women need to understand that men are very plain. Don't go reading between the lines." Ladies, take those words to heart. It will save you a lot of frustration and heartache.

When a woman marries, she is happy to think that her husband will be her one and only sexual partner. However, many guys get married thinking their spouse will not be the last woman they'll ever be with. He can't give up the hunt. "In the back of your mind you've always got to think that you just might have sex with Heather Locklear. A guy likes to feel that he's not locked in." It's not to say all men will cheat on their wives. Rather, they just have to feel they have that freedom. At the very least, as one man said, "I don't have an overwhelming desire to cheat on my wife, but I still leer at women and I love to see a gal without a bra."

When all was said and done about the why, when, and how to make a marriage work, the following stories were relayed to me by some husbands.

Mr. D, 36-years-old and the father of four children, "My wife and I were a few years into the marriage and sick of each other. We were arguing and it suddenly dawned on me why this was going on. I realized that I wasn't trying to win her heart anymore. Once I got her, I no longer did any of that. Nor did she, for that matter. We were in a slump. So, when I got a bonus check I handed it to her and told her to go out for the day with her girlfriends. I told her not to bring any presents home, and not to call home. I told her just to enjoy herself. When she came home she felt like she had had a 2 week vacation. She was beaming. A guy has to work to put his wife first. Our instinct is to put ourselves first, then the kids, and then the wife. I deliberately work at putting her first." Smart lad.

"Marriage does not exist on sex. It's about respect. The first three months you're the best lover in the world and then your wife becomes your mother. Passion goes in a marriage, but I love the safeness of it, the sense of home. When I had a massive heart attack three years ago I was lying in the emergency room thinking I was going to die. I was feeling okay because all I thought about was my responsibility to my wife and son. I was leaving them comfortable and they would be taken care of. My flock is all I have in my life."

Pleasing the female is not part of a boy's training. "The majority of men don't learn that part of the sexual pleasure comes from sharing and exchange. If you're lucky you'll learn it from your wife."

And finally, without hesitation, a 79-year-old told me the keys to a successful marriage:

1. Don't go to bed mad. Lean over and kiss your wife 2 or 3 times lovingly. Don't push your husband away.

2. Always make sure your differences have been resolved.

3. Don't be afraid to kiss your wife in a public place

4. Marriage is not a 50-50 proposition. Both have to be prepared to go 100%.

Chapter 6

INFIDELITY

"Some guys chase pussy forever. Few men want to stop chasing. If you're tired of the lies, chaos, confusion, and drama you'll eventually make some changes. I got tired of the 'clown game' and what it takes to keep up the charade. Flowers. Dinner. How do I keep her hooked? An affair has got to be reciprocal, but I don't want drama any longer. After I broke two or three hearts I realized the player game was too heartless. Or you stop chasing cause you're just not as appealing as you once were. The women 10 to 20 years younger than me are harder to get and most females my age, around 50, hold back because of what they've been through. It's not realistic anymore to chase because now you've got to show your health card. If there weren't STD's (sexually transmitted diseases) we'd probably chase a lot longer. When I was in my 30's I realized that it's not just about me. It's about a woman. The woman he's with helps him to settle down."

"You can have the most beautiful woman living with you, but the grass is always greener on the other side. A man wants to experiment, get that fix, but most men always come home." That pretty much sums up the story of infidelity.

"It's very easy for a guy to jump track. When a woman denies a man she is pushing him away. The attraction is gone. You've gotta have juice in your battery. You gotta stay charged, otherwise it don't run. If a wife starts to think differently of a husband he picks that up quickly. He might not talk about it because guys are not in touch with their emotions. They might not dwell on it in the conscious, but a guy will know it. It's like karate. You never show what you know because the opponent will use it against you." Do they come back? "It depends on the damage done."

Even if the female doesn't push the male away, he can easily 'jump track.' Case in point: one 75-year-old attorney, widowed and now remarried, spent the better part of the interview 'confessing' the sexual dalliances he had enjoyed during his 40 year marriage to his first wife whom he loved and never considered leaving for any of the other women. "I've never told anyone about my affairs", the first of which began after about twelve years of marriage, "not even my best friend who was also my doctor. I regard myself as a moral person. I was raised in a Methodist home. I couldn't even curse in front of my parents. I didn't drink or smoke. I was the high school valedictorian. I married at 21. We were both virgins. I yielded to temptation for the first time when I was 32. I wanted the women to be responsive and aggressive. I'd like to think women I had relations with didn't think I was taking advantage or mistreating them." He also spoke with tenderness describing the months he and his wife spent together and the closeness they developed in the months before she died of cancer. "I had the satisfaction of caring for my wife before she died. I remember with pleasure those last months. I thought back to the things we did. We rented videos, watched old movies together." As the interview progressed, the occasions on which he 'yielded to temptation' grew from a couple to more than a dozen. "Only one affair was emotional. I was in love with one women. I bought her a car and a piano. The affair ended when she married someone else." In spite of those dalliances, he regards himself as a moral person, but clearly said that if he had grown up later, specifically after the advent of the 60's 'sexual revolution' he didn't think he would have been "so moral". He also noted that once he had his first affair, it became easier to transgress. He did try a prostitute once, but "It was totally unsatisfactory. No affection. She wouldn't let me kiss her. I couldn't even get an erection. But the massage parlor was fun."

What doesn't work for one man can work for another. One never married 49-year-old doctor told me, "Prostitution can be very good for a marriage. It gives the man the sexual outlet that makes affairs of the heart less likely because the prostitute is unavailable and socially unacceptable. A guy has to have something more erotic than the woman who gave birth to his children, or the person with whom he's fighting over money." He was not without a sense of humor adding, "It should be part of every pre-nup! It's a safe relationship because it has to remain hidden. It's all acting, but to a guy it doesn't matter."

A little more crudely put by a 33-year-old twice divorced man, "Realize we're gonna be what we wanna be, and pretty much gonna do what we're gonna do. After the honeymoon, if the relationship is gonna work you then gotta work on it. Women need to realize going into a marriage that most men are schmucks. They're gonna stray, step out, quit opening the door, or buying roses."

From a 68-year-old who has been married for 47 years, "We know that women like fidelity in men, but we're not willing to take 100% of the responsibility for having an affair. Men have the reputation of straying, but I never made it with a girl that didn't want to make it with me. It took two of us and it was wonderful. And everybody got what they bargained for. Sometimes she got more out of it than I did. Men aren't the only schmucks because it takes two."

Sex for guys can be purely for the physical pleasure with no emotions. "Sex is not love. Sex is an animal desire which is better when love is involved. But it's still strictly a desire of the body. A guy can get sex anywhere and it can be all right, but not like if you care for her."

Emotionality continues to be forbidden territory for men. One 52-year-old, now in the midst of his second divorce, spoke with some pain, "If you're gonna have an affair, have a one night stand, then you won't get emotionally attached. If you get talking to a woman, you can get emotionally involved and that's bad news. I've been down that road before myself. I started to look during my first marriage cause I was on the road 18 years and when my wife wanted me to come home and work we had no relationship. I got emotionally involved, not so much sexually, with another woman and it turned out bad."

Are there signs that your partner is having an affair? Yes. A change in hairstyle, a change in the clothes he wears, working out, coming home late, no intimacy, paying no attention, and he wants a sports car.

What should a wife do if she learns her husband is cheating on her? "Survive the storm by making him aware that you know what's going on. A husband can have affairs and still love his wife. Don't be determined to punish. But if the infidelity persists, for her sake she should get out of the marriage. Try to understand, don't immediately make him pay. Marriage isn't about sex. A *real* schmuck is a guy that finds some chippy and leaves his family for her."

Yes, there is still a double standard. If a man found out that his wife is having an affair, the men's reactions were consistent, "I'd be greatly disturbed by it. It would undoubtedly eventually ruin the marriage. That's something a guy will never get over."

By now, much of what you've read may be begging the question of the 'gold standard' of infidelity – the mid-life crisis. Just what is it? "You get to a point when you think life is getting away from you. You think you haven't experienced everything that is available to you. It's not just sex. It's money. It's status. It's that mysterious time in life when men feel they must reach out beyond what their conventional life has to offer. Life is getting away from you. You're not as virile as you once were. You've been wondering for some time what it would be like to have a sexual experience with another woman." They feel cheated and want to make up for it. No matter what the cost. Or as a 41-year-old said, "Since the last 5 years or so, I've gotten to the point in life where I've got to tell things and let it out. I think that's a little earlier than most. I think most guys do it around 40 at the mid-life crisis."

"My mid-life crisis? Society has a lot to do with that. If you're not successful by 40 you're a failure. I bought a Porsche Turbo 951 when I was 38 during my divorce. I used to put my family first. And then I felt I no longer loved my wife. I had two daughters. I started to think about what can I do to make me happy. The turbo was addictive. It was like being shot out of a canon. Feel the power! I sat back and looked. It was one of those soul searching moments. What opened my eyes was a trip to the Philippines where I saw how others lived. It was humbling. I realized I didn't need all that. I searched my soul. What society told me is a lie. I had the same things I had before my midlife crisis, but life as it is is great and you start over."

A 74-year-old reflected, "There are lots of temptations out there. Especially a tank full of schmuckdom in your 40's. Women tempt men. They can be schmucks, too. Women at work have rubbed their breasts on me at the copy machine. If you're having a bad time at home, you're liable to say this is a good thing here at the office. I changed companies once to avoid that. I didn't tell anyone. Some guys want to prove that they're as bad as the other guys. Too many of us stray too early. A woman can control the sexual situation. She can say no. A woman has more control than she thinks she has."

One 17-year-old finds that most of his friends "...like being schmucks. They like to see how much they can get away with. They like to brag about cheating on their girlfriends."

"Men over a period of time do learn that right is better than wrong and do clean up their acts. **We outgrow our mid-life crises. We all heal.**"

Chapter 7

FRIENDSHIP BETWEEN GUYS: IT'S A BROTHERHOOD

Guys bond without talking. And it sounds like they have a sort of ready made kinship with each other because "We all already know we like the same things anyway." Those "same things" can be summed up with sports, women, mechanical things, and tools. **All men have the same basic wiring.**

The perfect world for a typical guy includes a big screen TV, going to football games, fishing or golfing with the guys, and hanging out with buddies. It's really that simple. "It's set up for us. You know it's the same way all over the world."

"A man views the world as a hierarchy. A woman finds value in knowing details about everything and other people. A guy finds value in status: car, house, job, money, and a beautiful woman on his arm. What's the first thing a guy will ask another guy at a cocktail party? 'What do you do?' Guys view the world as an organizational chart and try to figure out where they line up. It's a competitive thing."

Amidst this dog-eat-dog world, fishing and golf hold a Zen-like spell over most guys. Men can get dreamy-eyed talking about the love for and from a woman, but talking about fishing holds a close second when it comes to being spellbound. "I'm most relaxed when I'm fishing. Tomorrow my son and I are going fishing in the same boat my dad and I used 50 years ago. I love that boat. And we're going to the exact same spot where we fished."

"Men are not as articulate as females. So if the compatibility is right, guys bond without much talking." Ok, there's a little bit of talking when they hang out together. What does this look like? Well, there's sports, the stock market, and bragging. "They brag about everything. About breaking up, about sex. It's in their blood, they're born to brag." In terms of bragging about sex, they'll talk about the conquest, but not the particular woman. And they'll do anything to occupy themselves. That's where activities come in. "We don't sit around and compliment the clothes we wear or discuss the paint color in the bathroom."

Talk about not talking! One guy told me a story about his blithe reaction when he learned that a good friend from college got married. He didn't know about it until he read the wedding announcement in the paper. "I didn't care. But a woman would be hurt to learn about it that way."

There are two things guys *will not* talk about with other guys: secrets and emotional problems. "Secrets can show weaknesses. Nobody knows anything about me that is emotional. It shows too much weakness, and I don't want to sit and listen to that from other guys." The word 'weakness' came up over and over again whenever guys talked about emotions (including the emotion of love). Emotions = vulnerability = weakness.

What do they do with those secrets and emotions? "Well, they bottle them up and forget about them. If these feelings poke their ugly heads out men rebottle them and forget it again. A guy will be there for you with 'let's go get a beer, let's go fishing and forget about it. Let's go get another woman and forget about it. Let's get drunk, let's get laid'. And besides, guys don't need to download that often. We're programmed to keep it all in. **A guy can stew about something for years before he either lets it out or time obliterates it."**

Men know that women can empty out their feelings with other women. The male macho ego won't allow him to cry his eyes out in front of another guy – even his best, closest friend. "We envy that a woman can get her emotions out. Men don't show feelings because it makes us vulnerable and then they're afraid of getting attacked." The same gentleman went on to say that "We've forgotten that it's all right to be vulnerable. Most men don't know that vulnerability is a sign of strength."

Guys are primal and want to have freedom. They want to run and play like when they were little boys. "When you have kids you want to play with them because it's an excuse to play like when you were a kid. One of my best friends is an excavator. He's always smiling at work while operating the machinery because he gets to play in the dirt all day with the biggest toy."

"A guy doesn't give up freedom easily. A single guy has two faces: one for women and a second for his buddies. A married man has one face: one for the woman. When a guy is married he has to tell his wife he's going fishing. You do lose a certain amount of freedom." Take heed at these words, "There's a certain need for childish behavior throughout life...boys will be boys kind of stuff. You gotta let that happen. You don't know when it's gonna happen. There's the planned stuff like going boating or hunting. But there's also the spontaneous stuff, like going to a bar to play pool. You gotta open up the boundaries a little bit. Don't worry, they'll be back."

"If it seems that men want sex all the time, it's rooted in love and desire for the affection of the whole woman." The need for a woman is strong and powerful throughout a man's life. It's not just about physical pleasure for a man. Sex is intimately related to power and control. At the same time, the softness and feminine approach to life are elements he needs to be a complete male. Her soft, warm breath in his ear during love making brings a closeness between a man and a woman, confirms his masculinity and her love for and dependence upon him. Age has no effect on this phenomenon. "Men never get too old to think about sex. They may lose the physical ability, but not the mental ability." For simmering beneath the surface of the civilized man is his drive for sex. "It's key to our existence." Sex makes the world go 'round. It may go in a circle, but around nonetheless.

Since the beginning of time man has been impressed with what nature endowed him. The stories that follow confirm how barbaric attitudes and primitive feelings persist to this day. Understandable primitive feelings persist to this day. Understandable is the importance of a man's penis in life. When the young boy first finds himself with an erection, then an ejaculation, he is fascinated with his penis. "**Who loves the boy's penis the most? Himself.** Women don't fall in love with their sex organs. Men are walking phallic symbols." Young boys will form clubs. Hiking, swimming, fishing. Paralleling that will be the "Big Bat Game Club" where they compare sizes and marvel at their new bodily functions. As they grow older, and size continues to manifest itself, pride becomes a factor and a competitive thing. "It's the big pecker disease. It's like the 'five foot disease' in boating. You've always got to have the bigger boat. It's the same with the penis. You don't want to have the littlest one in the showers. Every guy in the locker room will notice the guy with the big dong."

There is no greater compliment than when his woman lovingly caresses him and in the heat of passion, tells him how beautifully big he is. "If a woman really wants to be complimentary she should always say how big and beautiful he is."

"In terms of sexual pleasure, a young man's primary interest is to ejaculate." A 54-year-old looked back, "My understanding of pleasure was my own ejaculation. **Pleasing the female is not part of a boy's training.** If you're lucky, you'll learn it from your wife. The majority of men don't learn that sexual pleasure is from sharing and exchange. Of course, the ultimate achievement is the ejaculation in the arms of a woman. But if I had a climax that resulted in pregnancy, so what? A young man has no clue that he has accountability for that. Pregnancy is life changing for a woman. They are given the privilege of having to be profoundly self-effacing. When you're pregnant, you're secondary. A woman is ready to sacrifice, to stand back and permit other realities to emerge." A 21-year-old confirmed the role of his age-appropriate sexuality, "Everything you do revolves around the 10 to 20 second period you are coming. Sex is 60-70% of a relationship. Everything else he does (fishing, etc.) is to bide time until he gets that sex again."

A woman who enjoys the deep love and warmth of a man's affection will invariably reciprocate by caressing his penis with her mouth. Reactions of the male to the intimacy and tenderness of a woman's lips is both sexually unbelievable and a true expression of the love they share. **"All men like oral sex.** I've never known a man who didn't. Guys like blow jobs because it's no effort and it's kind of cool to watch a woman suck your dick. If she swallows you are king of the jungle. It's about dominance. If a woman gives a great blow job she has ultimate power over a guy. It's absolute power over the male for a very, very short time. But every time she wants to come back she is more than welcome. She can continue to dangle that power."

There is nothing in a lover's caress more eroti-
cally stimulating or visually intimate than the caress
known as cunnilingus. A man finds there is no
greater thrill than feeling the moist softness, the
tender delicate skin, the pungent feminine scent a
woman releases as her body undulates in passion as
she takes the depths of his tongue into the folds of her
vagina. "Some women like oral sex to the extreme but
others won't allow it because they don't want to reciprocate. A lot of men don't know how to do it right,
but if they do a girl will follow you home."

Power and control were mentioned hand in
hand when sex was discussed. Sex is not just about
physical pleasure; for a man sex is related to power
and control. There's control over a woman (guys like
this a lot) as well as the power a woman can have
over the man (they don't like that as much). "If a
man can control a woman in the bedroom then he
can control her. If he can make a woman make that
sound he can control her. He doesn't have to hit,
threaten, or put her down. If you can touch a
woman's body from head to toe and make her feel
like a woman than you can control a woman.
Otherwise, they'll control themselves."

What does 'control' look like? "Control is
power. Power is when my girlfriend calls me at work,
leaves voice messages telling me where she is at all
times. She doesn't realize that I know that I got that

power because she calls me. I got the power over her. But you've got to control them in the bedroom first. It can be a curse, though. My girlfriend and I have a pretty good sex life. She doesn't want any other man. We do things together. But sometimes I can't go out of the house without her asking me what I'm doing."

"It's so true. The majority of men look at sex as control over women. It's because men fear the power of women. Men feel powerless in the presence of women who are in touch with who they are. **A man's salvation is in accepting his powerlessness and benefiting from what a woman has to offer.**"

In fact, if the woman is not interested in sex whenever the man wants it, it can leave him devastated. "We still think that when our mate doesn't desire us as much as we do her, then we get that mixed up with love. If my mate criticizes me or says any little thing it can crush me."

Sex. Vital to our existence. The cause of life, crimes of passion, the motivator of making money, and more confounding than the vastness of outer space. It means coitus. It means affection or love for someone.

For a guy sex and love are connected. Love for him, that is. Remember, as mentioned earlier, a guy can have affairs and it doesn't mean he doesn't love you. But don't even think that you can do the same. If he learns that his woman is having an affair, he may never get over that. All men agreed with this. **A guy has one set of standards for his sexual behavior and another set for her sexual behavior**.

"Take a young boy at 15. When he gets his first taste of sex he thinks he's in love. He wakes up at 18 or 20 realizing that sex is not love. They like the game."

"It's a double standard. If she went to bed with me I wonder who else. I wouldn't have married my wife if she wasn't a virgin. It's hard for a guy to think that she enjoyed it with somebody else. There is a double standard. A guy can think a woman is a slut if she sleeps with him. But the poor women have to accept 'that fucker ain't pure'. I'm so proud I was a virgin when I married. After a while women feel like they're being used. To a degree they are being used. Many men think women are good only for sex. You can wake up some of these young girls if you write this book." "If sex is too good than you think she's a slut. If it's not, then it's nothing...until you find the perfect woman for you. It gets better and better. It might stay the same, but it never gets old. And you can't wait to get back to her."

Believe it or not, men realize that women make the ultimate decision as to whether or not they will have sex. A thinking man, regardless of his desire for the woman, can appreciate when a woman says no. He may grump, groan, or protest, but deep inside he is aware of the possible consequences such as pregnancy and sexually transmitted diseases. "A woman has got to be in control of the sexual relationship. A man won't consciously acknowledge that part of the relationship. He feels it infringes on his masculinity. He will gladly acquiesce to the lust of a good sexual evening. A man can be a man very easily. A woman, as usual, is faced with the responsibility of guiding the relationship."

Chapter 9

WHAT TO LOOK FOR IN A MAN

When I asked men what advice they have for women, there was usually a pause before they spoke. And then they'd say things like, "That's a good question." And then there was another pause. They eventually told me a thing or two, but one gentleman later brought me a written response entitled "What Would I Look For in a Man" sub-divided into long-term and short-term relationships. I have done my best to keep the quirky things they've said along with some real profound ideas that every woman should think about as she looks for a life partner.

Sincerity and honesty were at the top of the list. "And how," I asked, "does a woman know about that in a guy?" Well, there is no quick cookbook answer. Time will tell you about his sincerity and honesty. "Give yourself time. You'll get all the answers to know someone's character." Don't overlook the clues that are given to you. The biggest mistake women can make is that they choose to overlook what they don't like about a guy thinking he is insincere or dishonest only now and then. Women think they can live with that. Wrong. Wrong. Wrong. And you know it. He does lousy things. He doesn't call when he says he will; he's unreliable. You will not be able to live with any of those behaviors. If you do it will eventually break your heart and you'll show up in my office sick with depression. Acknowledge it, move on, and take better care of yourself. Don't try to change his ways. It's impossible! How many times have I heard, "He's so cute. I thought I could help him. But he's impossible!"

Outward appearance. This is not about the cost of his clothes or whether you two have the same taste in dress. It's about how he takes care of himself. Is he clean? Are his fingernails dirty? Is he slovenly? Does he care about how he appears to himself, and to others? Is he overly concerned with his appearance, his clothes?

Bad habits. Does he drink? If so, moderately, excessively? If not, is it because he is in recovery? Does he smoke? If so, does it bother you? Does he use foul language? If so, does he apologize or is it a comfortable part of his vocabulary? A well-balanced man, sensitive to his surroundings, conducts himself accordingly.

Focus. Ask yourself, 'When we're on a date, does he look at me as if I'm the only woman there?' If he has a wandering eye that's a good sign that you should bolt. If he can't at least pretend this early in the game, chances are he never will.

Affection. If he says he loves you, but won't

hold hands in public, something is wrong. Shy men will accept affection. On the average, men show affection publicly. No compunction. He's proud; especially if the girl is pretty.

Conquer. Does it seem like you're the love of his life, or only something to conquer and move on to his next trophy? Be smart. This is not as hard to discern as you may think. Remember, love is blind. So be on your guard. Does he leave you love notes? Does he send you flowers? Does he look at you lovingly, with a dreamy face, with glassy eyes? You'll know it when you see it. If you don't think you've seen it, you haven't.

Money. How does he spend it? Does he live wildly or on a budget? Does he offer to pay for you? Is he generous with himself and only himself? Is his Porsche more important than you? A man reflecting those traits hasn't fully matured. You'll be raising a child.

Meet the family. Meet his parents. Many of your questions will be answered. Mothers and dads have a great influence on how their children turn out. One man, when he asked to meet his future wife's step-dad was told, "'Hell, no, I don't want to meet that SOB!' I knew then that I was competition."

Siblings. Is he an only child? It might mean that he's a brat. This is harsh, but this is what guys told me. It also means you'll be expected to fulfill the impossible conditions created by his doting parents and loving relatives. What were his female influences growing up? Does he have sisters? If he has younger sisters, he's likely been the protector. If he has older sisters, he's probably been bossed around. Either way, the more women he's been around, the more well-rounded he'll be. He'll be more accepting of female whims, changing moods, PMS, and other seemingly difficult and unpredictable behaviors.

Education. How much and what kind? A marriage is based on friendship, respect, affection, compatibility...not education. No level of learning tells us how to live with another.

Occupation. What does he do for a living? Does he love his work? If he does, it brings happiness to all facets of life.

Marriage. Is he married? If not, has he been married and does he want to be? If you're interested in getting married let him know this early on. If you're looking for a life partner don't spend time with players.

Does he have children? Ask.

What are his plans for the future? Ask.

Do you have common interests? A man shares what he likes with the woman he loves. He doesn't usually ask if she likes it or not. The more you have in common the smoother its going to be. Can you accommodate? Are you willing to do things with him just to make him happy? Would you drive two hours to a football game and sit through it only because he wants your company? Would he return the favor?

On the other hand, if you're just out for a short-term romp with a guy here are the simple ingredients:

Is he good looking?
Do you like the way he dresses?
Do you like his taste in cars?
Does he even have a job?
Does he still live at home?
How much does he spend on a date?
What does he like to do on a date?

And finally, if you don't want to bother at all you may agree with the words from a 50-year-old thrice married and divorced guy who told me he was depressed because he had left his second wife years ago for a "slut of a third wife" and he now wants his second wife back.

"Why d'ya do that?" I asked.

"Cause I'm an asshole," he replied without hesitation.

"You know, I'm writing a book about guys – why are you guys such assholes?"

Again, without hesitation, he said, "I don't know. If I knew I'd be writing the book."

"Well, let me ask you something else, what advice do you have for women?"

"Stay away from us! They make replaceable parts

that you can slap around and they don't talk back!"

Dear reader, this information is all yours.
Take your time.

ARE WE FROGS IN BOILING WATER?

No matter what their ages or origins there isn't a guy alive who hasn't done schmucky things. The younger guy is in the midst of doing these very things. The older guy knows his schmuckdom days are in the past. Characteristically, no man was proud of being a schmuck.

And as men reflected on themselves they also looked at the world today and the influences that contribute to their schmuckiness. "The single most serious affliction is that young men don't know who they are. Most are not given the privilege and opportunity to discover their true selves because cultural patterns are imposed on boys. Specifically, today's culture tells boys that they haven't achieved anything of significance if they haven't succeeded in a very narrow range of behaviors: athletics, domination, whatever is the opposite of humility. And everything in this society is cast as win or lose."

"I think there is a real crisis in masculinity now. Guys are not as nice as they used to be. One of the biggest mirrors of cultural schmuckdom is what is reflected in our own media. Look at the violence in TV and movies. Men do suffer identity crises in this society. Masculinity has been misunderstood. **Genuine masculinity is strength under control.** The current male model is strength out of control. We don't know what true masculinity looks like."

"The vast majority of guys are schmucks and most are not aware of it because to have the schmuck mentality is what the media presents so it's cool to be that way. 'Pimp' is a catchword for having a way with ladies that's considered a good thing. There's a club where I go to college and they had a 'Pimps & Ho's Night'. The image of masculinity is becoming more and more extreme. It's buying into the false belief that men and women are opposites – i.e., man is strong, female is weak. That men have to be aggressive towards women and have more confidence than they really have. Look at Howard Stern's show. It's degrading to women. He's acts like a cave man and yet they say he's on the cutting edge. He's always asking women to undress. A lot of guys think he's cool."

"Rap music is now mainstream. At best, women are called chicks or babes, but usually bitches. Black women are called ho's. And women are buying into it. Society is completely centered on sex. Look at the body piercing, tattooing. This culture is becoming more fascinated by it. Pornography is degrading to women because it's about dominating women. This stuff is becoming more acceptable. Look at TV after 9pm. Ask any guy about "Girls Gone Wild". It's more prevalent and it's no longer a big deal because we're saturated. Now with the Internet, anyone has access to an adult book store."

"It's like putting a frog in boiling water. He'll jump right out. But put a frog in warm water that is slowly heating up and he'll stay in it. Once it's boiling he can no longer handle it but he doesn't know to jump out. He's gotten so used to it that he doesn't know he's in danger and will die."

"The value of a man is based on his ability to dominate others, to not show feeling, and to have sexual prowess. Women are taught their greatest asset is their body and their value is based on their sex appeal. What are the differences between men and women? Women are more nurturing, but it's a behavior that men can learn. I think the differences are subtle and that our society magnifies them." "Men and women are different, but that's a good thing. We want to attack our differences. We should, instead, see them as complementary, not as contradictory."

"Men are up against very few role models. Having been in the Army and college, I've seen that men will make notoriously sick plans in order to dominate or control. It's historic and it's global. The whole European heritage is profoundly about this. The dominant theme is control and exploit. If you succeed in controlling you have the green light to exploit."

"Most men live in the absence of moral leadership. Moral leadership for women is a collective observation – women doing things together. Yes, that's moral leadership. Individual women emerge in articulating the collective consciousness. Young men are taught that 'you've got to do it yourself.' You're not taught that it's a collective enterprise requiring cooperative action. Women understand that they can't make it alone. It's modeled for them."

"We don't have to be this way," became a common, spontaneous theme that was spoken by several of the men 50 years and older. It wasn't with harshness or regret that they said this. Nor did I feel that guys were trying to convince me of anything. There was an aura of thoughtfulness about them. "Men are seriously handicapped in their ability to express emotion. I'm talking Neanderthal man and women are adapting to that. In fact, **women are acquiring the weakest male attributes.** We don't have to be this way. There is so much injury that people don't know they're abused. Guys would like to be different, they just don't know how. We can be controlled by love or fear. Most guys are controlled by fear."

And I was asked, "Do you think there's a guy around who hasn't abused a woman?" And, "Do you think a man can covet a non-sexual relationship with a woman?"

Guys taught me something very important about being a woman. I learned that men adore and envy us for our wonderful feminine qualities of nurturing and loyalty. This makes us remarkable and powerful creatures in men's hearts. As women have advanced in their material, educational, and professional worlds, perhaps, we have yet to value and incorporate those uniquely feminine qualities in our relationships with men. And, once we do, perhaps we'll see fewer and fewer schmucks around us.

THE CHALLENGES OF KNOWING GUYS: NOW IT'S UP TO YOU

So you've survived life's little wisdoms garnered from the experiences of many. To top off what you've sweated through, keep in mind the following:

- Be patient.

- Women make too much out of men…they are not that complicated.

- Don't be afraid to ask, "Why?"

- Be forgiving, persevering, and guiding. But don't let him know you're teaching. Don't point out his faults.

- A man may not understand a woman. Just because he's attentive doesn't mean he understands.

- Don't expect your husband to be your girlfriend.

- Keep your girlfriends. They will be your life long emotional supports.

- Men are insecure about being exposed as weak or shameful. When they're insecure they become defensive, demanding, and they disconnect.

- Be healthy. If you're not healthy without a man, you'll never be healthy with a man. A man will not make a woman healthy. He will exploit her unhealthy areas in an effort to control this woman who has become a part of his life.

- A woman is vital to a man.

- Men are only human beings. There are no knights in shining armor or Prince Charmings.

- Look for someone to complement you, not define you.

- Men are afraid of intimacy, but they desire it (with a wife) more than anything else.

- Men are warriors (women are worriers). When they feel vulnerable, they go into battle mode and attack!

- Love him unconditionally, but don't use that as an excuse to stay in an abusive relationship. Love him for who he is, not for what you think he can be.

- Things get better by the time guys reach 60... "The testosterone calms down and we become more accomodating."

- No matter how schmucky a guy is, it's all about the woman.

- Don't be afraid to let him know that you know that Guys are Schmucks! You'll be pleasantly surprised at his response.

INTERVIEWEES

Age 17, student, never married

Age 17, student, never married

Age 22, college student, never married

Age 22, electrician/security guard, engaged

Age 33, unemployed, twice divorced

Age 36, pharmaceutical representative, married

Age 40, contractor, married

Age 40, minister, married

Age 45, psychologist, married

Age 46, psychologist, never married

Age 49, physician, never married

Age 50, plant manager, married

*Age 50, office worker/musician, once married
     and divorced*

Age 52, truck driver, twice divorced

Age 52, program manager, twice married,
    once divorced

Age 53, retired laborer, once married
    and divorced

Age 54, professor, married

Age 55, carpenter, thrice divorced

Age 57, physician, twice married, once divorced

Age 58, physicist, thrice married, twice divorced

Age 60, record company president, twice married,
    once divorced

Age 61, bus driver, married

Age 68, retired public relations executive, married

Age 74, realtor, married

Age 75, attorney, twice married, once widowed

Age 79, engineer, married

Age 80, entertainer, married

Age 85, retired writer/producer, twice married,
    once divorced

Printed in the United States
24391LVS00001B/328-345

9 781583 850558